THE

TRUTH

ABOUT

MAGIC

THE

TRUTH

ABOUT

MAGIC

ATTICUS

poems

ST. MARTIN'S GRIFFIN
New York

First published in the United States by St. Martin's Griffin, an imprint of St. Martin's Publishing Group

THE TRUTH ABOUT MAGIC. Copyright © 2019 by Atticus Publishing, LLC. All rights reserved. Printed in the United States of America. For information, address St. Martin's Publishing Group, 120 Broadway, New York, NY 10271.

www.stmartins.com

Photographs by Bryan Adam Castillo Photography, Poppet Penn, Ramón Laguía, or released under Creative Commons Zero license

The Library of Congress Cataloging-in-Publication Data is available upon request.

ISBN 978-1-250-23281-6 (trade paperback)

ISBN 978-1-250-23279-3 (hardcover)

ISBN 978-1-250-26685-9 (signed)

ISBN 978-1-250-23280-9 (ebook)

Our books may be purchased in bulk for promotional, educational, or business use. Please contact your local bookseller or the Macmillan Corporate and Premium Sales Department at 1-800-221-7945, extension 5442, or by email at MacmillanSpecialMarkets@ macmillan.com.

First Edition: September 2019

10 9 8 7 6 5 4 3 2 1

This book is dedicated to Alina.

A girl I never knew

who died in my arms.

This book is for
the day dreamers,
the night thinkers,
the summer skinny dippers
for anyone who ever said
"the night is young"
or watched the sunrise
on a beach
far from home—
but mostly
it's for you
the quiet ones
at parties
looking out of windows
wondering about the stars.

xx Atticus

MAGIC

IN

YOUTH

*Children see magic
because they look for it.*
—Christopher Moore

"I don't know many things
with any certainty,"
she said
"but snuggling feels important."

Our lips barely left each other
in those first few weeks
only enough breath
to gasp for life
and then back
into the tangle of it all
the unlockable knot of new love
and that faint perhaps
of the forever-be.

She wanted what every young heart wanted
for something beautiful to find her beautiful.

Love exists
somewhere between
a girl pretending
she can't open a jar of pickles
and a boy pretending
not to know she could.

ATTICUS

We reveled
in the sweet taste of each other's names
as if honey was a sound
and we were thirsty
for its song.

We tangled in bedsheets
skateboarded in rainstorms
and rode subways to jazz clubs
you were an actress
and we were a film
and like all good movies
we ended in love
credits down kissing
to sunsets under Brooklyn bridges.

She fell for the idea of him
and ideas were
dangerous things to love.

He was one of the bad boys
the smoldering kind
that smokes cigarettes
and drinks whiskey
right out of the bottle—
the kind
you can't keep past sunrise
and you don't really care.

We just want
the world to love
the little monsters
that we are.

If I'm honest,
very little in life
has compared
in immensity
or magnitude
before or since
to the electric
and wild feeling
of the first time
I kissed
a girl.

One of those forever kinds of friends
where anything can happen
and nothing will change—
they just always are
and forever will be.

We were all born to live
born to love
millions of years
perfecting the art of it,
and yet still,
somehow,
it comes so unnaturally
to most of us.

ATTICUS

All I dream
is for our shadows
to spend
a little
more forever
together.

We grow old chasing the truths
we knew as children.

I love you
he said
to the end of all things
and on—
and she smiled
soaking
in the infiniteness
of it all.

We aspire
only to live
our lives well,
to fall into the gentle to and fro of life,
and the refrains of seasons and tides
rocking us slowly & finally to sleep
as old and loved
as we can possibly be.

Have you ever had a feeling
there's more to you
than the person
everybody else sees
a person hidden deep within
the very fabric of your soul—
you must pull that thread
unravel the truth of you
and wake within yourself
that great giant
you already know
you can be.

MAGIC

IN

LOVE

Magic will find those with pure hearts, even when all seems lost.
—Morgan Rhodes

LOVE
WAITS FOR ALL OF US
QUIETLY
IN THAT PLACE
WHERE NO ONE
IS LOOKING.

We were far
too in love
with being in love
to care.

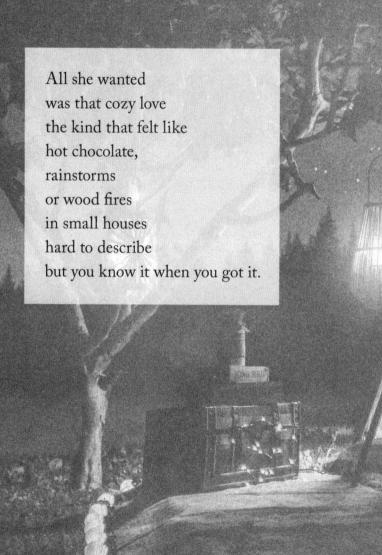

All she wanted
was that cozy love
the kind that felt like
hot chocolate,
rainstorms
or wood fires
in small houses
hard to describe
but you know it when you got it.

It takes almost all of me
not to always kiss you always.

All I wish
is for you
to one day
love you
the way
I do.

True love happens at the edge of all things
a lavender place between wake & sleep.

We fall in love
with the little things
somebody loves
about the world
like music,
rainy days,
or peanut butter sandwiches—
and it doesn't matter
what they are,
it's just that they love them
and that makes us happy.

We all know the rules of love
we know we shouldn't chase
we know we should play it cool
we know we shouldn't say
those ridiculous things we say
but we do them anyways
because the truth is
we can't really help it
and we don't really want to.

To be honest
you scare me
I'm terrified of letting you in
of seeing myself
more clearly through your eyes
wondering if I'm good enough
or if one day I'll lose you
but the truth is
not having you at all
scares me more
than all the other
truths of love
and that thought
makes me brave.

Many of us are cursed
to never let ourselves believe
another person could love us—
and we will slowly
drown our love
in that confusion.

I don't need to matter to everyone
but I do need to matter to someone.

She didn't make
my demons disappear
she made me
strong enough
to fight them.

When I first met you
I remembered you
from a hundred different dreams
and there you were
for me to love
all over again
for the very first time.

There will always be that moment
when we look at someone
for the first time in love with them.

Indifference is a powerful tool of desire.

What a grand
and beautiful force
the immense
and wildly unappreciated
power of
human touch.

"Your sweater smells like you,"
she said
"I wish it were a magic sweater
so when I took it off
and shook it
you would arrive into it
just like magic—
I hate sweaters that aren't magic."

We've moved on now
but if
I'm honest
I am still
a little bit
in love
with all the ways
we were.

Sometimes
even great love
is not enough.

I don't know the meaning of life,
but kissing a girl
while drunk in the rain
   is pretty damn close.

The simplest truth
is that we
fall in love with the way someone
makes us feel or doesn't
and that's pretty well
the all of it.

You have robbed me
of all heart & mind
and I love you
sweet bandit of my soul.

In the right love
we will discover new love for ourselves.

IT'S ALWAYS BEEN HIM

SHE SMILED

OUR SOULS JUST *DANCE* THE SAME.

I find more love
in a storm
with you
than a thousand
sunny days without.

When they met
they were old already,
and so could skip
all the awkward parts of love,
realizing that neither was perfect
and never would be
instead they met as two old souls
worn well from a life of true moments
and together
they lingered
in each other's last few shadows
soothing scars
from a life well lived.

"What a beautiful thought,"
she said,
"that even death does not conquer love
and sometimes even makes it stronger."

MAGIC

IN

ADVENTURE

*Magical places are always beautiful
and deserve to be contemplated.*
—*Paulo Coelho*

There's something magic
about airports
it's like standing in a room
with a thousand doors.

I like the way Paris tastes on my tongue,
it's all fancy and full of bubbles.

I LIKE TO THINK GOD SMILES
AT SOME OF HER BEAUTIFUL SUNSETS.

ATTICUS
◆◆

I had the aching feeling I always got
when I stayed in a place too long
my bones became restless beneath my skin
like I'd forgotten how to run
I longed only for the great new
and so,
I packed my bags and
stepped out onward
toward the dusty roads
of tomorrow
and the never been.

*The art to traveling
is uncovering the hidden treasures
a country didn't know
they hid.*

There is no safer place I know
than hidden
among
the rattling old bones
of Brooklyn
in a storm.

We ran from beach clubs
in rain showers
drinking champagne from bottles
jumping into pools in our clothes
and kissing under lightning,
we yelled promises
in thunderclaps
to never grow old—
and I fell in love
with you
and the absolute certainty
it all would last forever.

Wine will make fools of us all
the dosage just varies.

She was that kind of friend
that after one drink
would have you
signing up for hip-hop classes,
ordering bottles of tequila
to other people's tables,
and planning how
to move to France.

Say what you will
but crazy isn't boring.

I wish
I was a spicy margarita
so I could be
adored
by you
forever, often
and abundantly.

She wasn't looking for the perfect person
she was looking for someone
to catch her imagination
and remind her what she was looking for.

I am alive in the breath of Rome,
my soul
a thousand years awake
and born today.

Swimming pools were invented
to kiss girls in the rain
and if they weren't
they should have been.

You're
a
tall
pour
of half
drunk
whiskey
my
pigeon-
toed
gypsy.

Give me a room in Paris
the smaller, the better
and it must be winter
and it must be cold
so we can make it hot
too hot to sit still
and the window must be thin
so we can hear the bells
and the power must surge and bubble
so the lights flicker
and the records skip
let the water be weak
so our coffee is strong
so we can stay up late to dance.
Give me this Paris
and I will paint for you
all the truths I know
about magic.

ATTICUS

Oh no,
I've had the slow murmur of a Paris thought,
the kind that won't leave
until well after
a month-long-week
of rosé,
cafés,
and sunsets on the Seine.

We visited old markets
selling ancient glories
from Ozymandian dreams
we'd dress up in furs
and fancy hats
and have dinners at long tables
until kindly asked to leave
and then to some café somewhere
in a place that didn't matter
drinking rosé
and eating spiced olives
until we'd stumble to our beds
this was our life
everything that mattered
everything that
would ever matter
and we lived each day
as a season of our spring.

Wine so delicately
pulls from us
all the stories
we hadn't planned to tell.

Travel and love
are worth the sacrifice
for a life without them
is a life unexplored.

*The melancholies of all existence
are quickly forgotten in a walk around Rome.*

ATTICUS

You'll never hear
the old man say
that he wished he didn't
see the world
and had
more money
when he died.

The way you flirt with Paris
I am forgotten
left in the spinning blossom
of your love—
and all I can do is
watch you both
and smile
as the gardens bloom.

Let's stop
pretending
to be so perfect
for the world
and get on
with finding out
if we can be
so perfect
for each other.

The way he talked of their dreams
it made her want to grab his hand
and run quickly into their tomorrows.

My darling,
let's you and I
ramble on this life awhile—
our hands in hands
our hearts in hearts
our shadows forever one.

MAGIC

IN

HER

She's mad, but she's magic.
There's no lie in her fire.
—Charles Bukowski

CHANCES ARE
YOU ARE
SOMEONE'S
GIRL NEXT DOOR.

She was a queen
safe and unconquerable
in the wild
walled kingdoms
of herself.

*Life with her became
a divine linger between kisses.*

ATTICUS

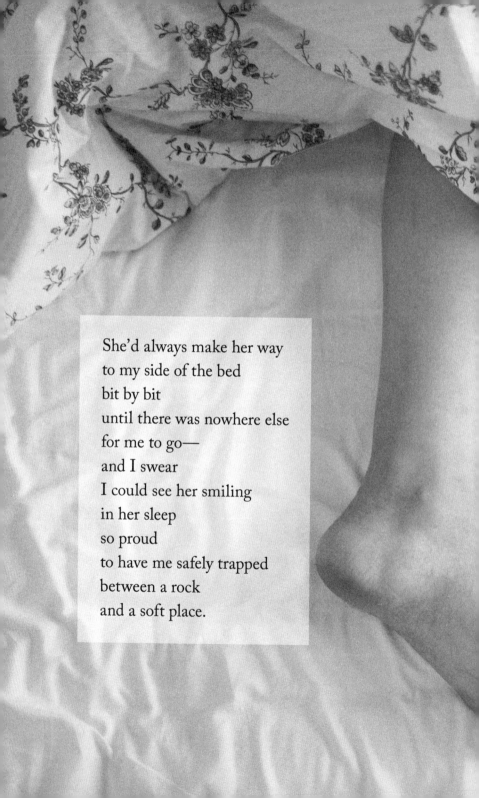

She'd always make her way
to my side of the bed
bit by bit
until there was nowhere else
for me to go—
and I swear
I could see her smiling
in her sleep
so proud
to have me safely trapped
between a rock
and a soft place.

I like you
just the way you are—
in my baggy shirts
in my tangled sheets
eating popcorn in my bed
quietly
so I don't hear you.

He loved those wrinkles around her eyes
little reminders of their life well laughed.

I'll forever kiss you
in public places
people can hate it
if they like
I don't mind
I'd still rather the kisses.

The sex was a bonus
to the great and wondrous privilege
of being in close proximity
to her jokes.

He traced
her silhouette
with moonlight
and found in the stars
the calligraphy
of her soul.

She had an uncanny energy for life
thankful for every little miracle it bestowed—
and it made her
    entirely impossible
    to live without.

She was a storm
the kind of girl
you needed to lose
yourself to find
somewhere
up half a bottle of whiskey
and down half the moon of sky.

She kept coming back to me
like smoking
or drinking
or any of those other
bad habits
that eventually
try to ruin you.

She was just another fool in love
with cities,
boys
and gods.

The greatest lie
he ever told
was that she needed him
to be happy.

She wasn't looking for a fairy tale
just to feel a little less lonely.

Cheer up, beautiful
you'll be in love again
and probably sooner
than you're ready.

In her heart
and soul
she set fire to all things
that held her back
and from the ashes
she stepped
into who she always was.

And,
out of her
great sorrow
and fear,
came one
exhilarating
seed of
thought
that consumed
her in a calming
wave of love and hope—
she was free.

She stood there
bathing in the grand forests of his love
with only the quiet rustle
of the treetops against the sky
to remind her she was real at all.

SOME GIRLS

LOOK GOOD IN DIAMONDS,

SOME GIRLS

MAKE DIAMONDS LOOK GOOD.

I feel in every girl
there lives
a wild pixie,
that if let go,
would run and dance in grassy fields
until the end of the world—
and when that girl grows up,
that pixie hides,
but she's always there,
peeking out behind old eyes
and reading glasses,
waiting
to one day dance again.

Somewhere
in the great landscape of time
there is a garden growing
the most beautiful rose
that has ever been
and that will ever be—
you are that rose,
forever to me.

*I'll forever chase
the girls
like you
that make
me feel
a little more
like me.*

"When do I know
if I really love her?"
asked the boy
and the old man smiled,
"When it's no longer
a question."

MAGIC

IN

DARKNESS

The world is full of magic things, patiently waiting for our senses to grow sharper.

—W. B. Yeats

She reminded me of dusk
and the inevitable fading
of all beautiful things.

*We don't need every dream to come true—
sometimes we just need to dream them for a while.*

Don't waste
a second
of your time
convincing
other people
you're worth
loving.

It was the end of love
and beginning of truth
as if
the first time they ever met
was the day they said good-bye.

We lay there within the lonely silence of all the things we didn't say.

They are fools,
you know—
those ones who think
you can never change
those ones who think
you can never grow—
for as long as you live
you will have today
to prove them wrong.

You stole pieces of me
in all the love I gave you
and never got back.
Keep it now
it is my gift to you
for you will not get more—
and that,
my love,
is my gift to me.

No good lust goes unpunished.

Beware
the fair-weather lover
who is everything for you
as long as it is easy.

No
life isn't that bad
just today
today sucks
today's the f*king worst
but probably not tomorrow
or even the next day
yeah,
the next day might be f*king sweet.

Our love had become
a dream
fading from us
no matter how hard
we closed our eyes.

My lonliness loves the rain.

So often, we punish ourselves with the bad love we think we deserve.

She wasn't happy or sad,
in love or out of love,
she was just there
existing
in the ebb and flow of life—
and that was a dangerous place to be
but her worst mistake
was forgetting to remember
there was more.

When given a choice
between you and them
choose you.
It's better to be whole and alone
than broken at their feet.

Misery at least makes good art.

I LOVE PEOPLE

BUT WOW

DO

I

ALSO

LOVE

NO PEOPLE.

His was a selfish love
patching
his soul
with all
of her pieces.

You will find
that most of life's
toughest
and more existential
questions
can be solved
or indefinitely postponed
by spending more time
around the people you love.

It's too sunny today.
I just need you, some blankets and a storm.

Death is only dangerous
to the unlived life.

People,
like diamonds,
become
less perfect
the closer
you get
the trick is
to not forget how they shine.

Obsessions are nine tenths of my flaws.

Mirror
mirror
on
the
wall
tell
no
more
lies
of
who
we
are.

Don't hide from heartbreak
for it will show you more truth
than a thousand happy days
live in it, soak in it
and let it evolve you
into your next and greater form.

Sometimes,
it's the ones that seem to love themselves
the most
that actually love themselves the least.

HOW BEAUTIFUL YOU ARE

HE SAID

A TAPESTRY OF SCARS.

It's good to be with someone
who has been through hell—
life is hard,
and strange,
and a lot of shit happens.
And when someone's been through the
worst of it already,
pain doesn't come as much of a surprise,
they just
sit down
tie their shoelaces
wave to old demons,
and get on with it.

You think you are alone
but you're not
we are here
and a million others too
all scared
all confused
all worried it might never change
but here is the big secret
the one they don't tell you
you're doing it right
just by living,
and everything
will be okay.

MAGIC

IN

WORDS

Books are a uniquely portable magic.
—Stephen King

Poetry at the wrong time is madness
poetry at the right time is magic.

People will say you're beautiful
but it takes a special person
to make you believe it.

We are much more useful to the world
in forgiving ourselves
than hating ourselves.

Whiskey is like poet's water.
It quenches our thirst for madness.

ATTICUS

I begged the universe
for you
and one day
you arrived
as everything I'd always
asked for
and it didn't take me long
to realize—
I should have been
more specific.

Today I opened a book
and found a flower
that you'd pressed—
it was orange
and red
and yellow
and small.
And in all ways
it was our love
gone now
but beautiful still
as the memory of something more.

To a poet,
the broken flowers
bloom the brightest.

I am so many mountains more
than the way
you make me feel.

Wine
is the poetry
I read on weekends.

I don't want to send clever texts anymore,
can you just love me?

Bookstores
are wormholes
to all the
could-have-beens,
the has-beens,
and all the maybe-be's.

The way you look
when you sleep
is the perfect secret
whispered only
to me.

Don't move an inch
in this morning light
should you smudge
the beautiful I see
I want to paint you
every curve with words
and place you
on the mantle of my soul
as the forever memory
of dawn.

Poets spend their whole lives
trying to think
of a better way to say,
"He loved a girl."

I am fine to be alone
but sometimes
I find myself missing what it is
to miss someone.

We resent our parents
for all our worst faults
and they in turn
resent theirs,
and so too back
to the slugs of primordial soup
who resented their parents
for giving them legs.

If I conquered all my demons
there wouldn't be much left of me.

He was a brother
I never had,
different than the others,
and he carried in his eyes
and on his arms
the tattoos
and scars
of being famous young,
he wore the face
of a star
but all I saw
was a poet
drowning
in someone else's dreams
who wished only
to sink
into the quiet sea
or fade
into any painted wall of Brooklyn.

Don't believe everything you know for sure.

Your scars
are not your shame
he said
they are your story,
and I love stories.

Mix our pages
bleed our ink
write your story into mine
so there are
no beginnings
and no ends
just pages of us
and the always will be.

I shivered when I wrote it
she shivered when she read
what ghost is this
that follows words
into my lover's head?

I've had a million "likes"
and one loving hand in mine
and let me assure you—
love is in the latter.

A poet
journeys
only to
understand
the great truths hidden in all of us:
of what is love,
and why?

MAGIC

IN

STARS

Magic exists. Who can doubt it, when there are rainbows and wildflowers, the music of the wind and the silence of the stars?

—*Nora Roberts*

The truth about magic
lies in the very
perfect fading wish
of every shooting star.

ATTICUS

You and I
are stars
met once
in the breath of a universe
crossed only for a moment
as the ebb and flow
of dust and atoms.

Some say
the sun is god—
and you don't see
the sun
minding
who it warms.

She took stamps
from the drawer in the kitchen
her father saw but didn't say
they drove
and she watched out the window
fingering them carefully
in her pocket
together they climbed the grassy hill
up to the acorn tree
stopping at a rock
perfectly carved
with a woman's name—
for a long time
and a careful time
she looked and thought
but never cried.
"Papa?"
she finally said,
"How many stamps
does it take to reach heaven?"
"One will do,
my love—"
And so,
she put one stamp on
and placed one inside
and left the letter
by her mother's side.

ATTICUS

Sometimes,
you have to be quiet
to really see the stars.

ATTICUS

What a perfect sound,
he said,
that laugh,
like when the sun warms
your face through the clouds.

I have noticed
that all wine
regardless of the cost or vintage
tastes the same when sipped
directly out of the bottle
running naked to the beach
under a full
and summer moon.

Let's trade our tomorrows
for the champagne and
the stars tonight

Keep your kingdoms
give me only
the open road
the stars in the sky
the smell of a campfire
around the next bend
and I will be as rich as any king.

I have noticed
through careful observation
that you look your best
soaked in champagne
under fireworks
dancing in the rain.

ATTICUS

On those nights
when the thick snow drifts
through moonlight
and the sky looks like falling stars
close your eyes
look up
tongue out to the gods
and feel the cool ash burn you.

I sit on clouds and obsess
with angels
when I should be obsessing
on the fact I can fly.

Each beautiful thing
we love
starts first as the dirt
of dust
and
stars.

ATTICUS

Billions of years of evolution
perfecting the ecstasy
of a lover's first touch.

She loved quiet nights mostly
but that night
she wanted to
drink tequila,
kiss girls with soft lips
and have a mysterious boy
with a dark complexion
take her to a rooftop
and tell her interesting things about the stars.

We humans
are flowers
bloomed only to die.
But we are beautiful still
in the gardens that we've made.

Somewhere
sitting on a cloud
deep in the sky
there is a secret list
written by an angel
that holds
all the wonderful moments
your life
has yet to come.

I hold
my breath
for love
or death
or whichever
comes sooner.

*For how hard life can be
it will be sad to see it go.*

"Seems a shame to leave now"
the old man said
"I was just getting the hang of things."

And as the moons of youth
spilled once more into dawn
we found ourselves infinite again—
if only for a moment.

The truth is—magic lives in all of us who choose to look for it.

It lives in the morning in the springtime, it's in the smell of the world after the rain, or a stormy afternoon in bed on a Sunday, it's in warm sweaters and a lovers' nook, it's in those days that never end, and the days that end too soon.

It's in every spicy margarita or bathtub with rosé, it's in good books and Spanish beaches, it's in forests where the trees sway or lakes that shine back the moon.

It's in art; it's in music; it's in words. It's in you and it's in me and any of us that choose to find it. For the greatest truth about magic...is that it's true.

xx Atticus

ATTICUS

ACKNOWLEDGMENTS

Thank You:
Sarah Cantin
Andrea Barzvi
My Gogo
Spencer Roehre
Poppet Penn
Bryan Adam Castillo
Penni Thow
David Lingwood
Karlie Kloss
Joey Parris
Marissa Daues
Mom, Dad, brothers & sisters
Lindsay O'Connell
Ramón Laguía
The cities of Paris and Rome
Emma Roberts & Karah Preiss, Shay Mitchell

And, to all my readers. This book was made for you.

To everyone at SMP:

Jennifer Enderlin
Anne Marie Tallberg
Brant Janeway
DJ DeSmyter
Meghan Harrington
Clare Maurer
Rachel Diebel
Kerri Resnick
David Stanford Burr
Nicola Ferguson
Sally Richardson
Andrew Martin

Thank You,
xx
Atticus